W9-BNB-097

MERCURY

A TRUE BOOK

by
Larry Dane Brimner

Children's Press®
A Division of Grolier Publishing

New York London Hong Kong Sydney
Danbury, Connecticut

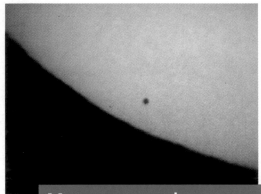

Mercury can be seen as a tiny dot as it orbits around the Sun.

Subject Consultant
Peter Goodwin
Science Department Chairman
Kent School, Kent, CT

Reading Consultant
Linda Cornwell
Learning Resource Consultant
Indiana Department
of Education

Author's Dedication:
For my friends at
Lantern Lane
Elementary School

Visit Children's Press® on the Internet at:
http://publishing.grolier.com

Library of Congress Cataloging-in-Publication Data

Brimner, Larry Dane.
    Mercury / by Larry Dane Brimner.
        p.   cm. — (A true book)
    Includes bibliographical references and index.
    Summary: Describes the orbit, rotation, temperature, and surface for-
mations of the planet Mercury and the probe Mariner X that took
pictures of it in 1974 and 1975.
    ISBN 0-516-20619-2
    1. Mercury (Planet)—Juvenile literature. 2. Space flight to Mercury—
Juvenile literature. [1. Mercury (Planet)] I. Title. II. Series.
QB611.B75 1998
523.41—dc21   97-38648
                                                                CIP
                                                                AC

© 1998 by Larry Dane Brimner
All rights reserved. Published simultaneously in Canada
Printed in the United States of America
1 2 3 4 5 6 7 8 9 10 R 07 06 05 04 03 02 01 00 99 98

Contents

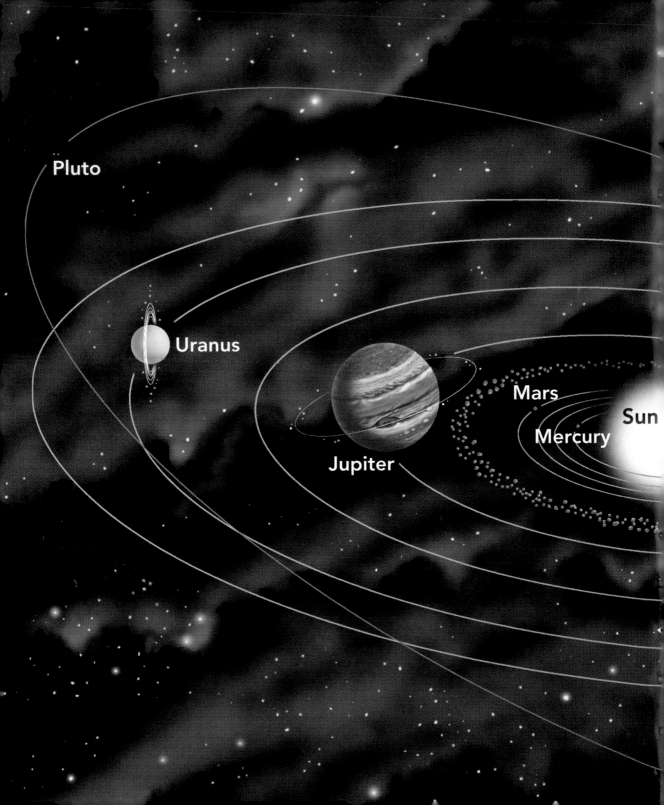

The Solar System

Venus

Moon

Earth

Asteroid Belt

Saturn

Neptune

 A Puzzle

Much of our solar system is a puzzle. How were the Sun and nine planets formed? Why is there life on Earth but not on the other planets? What are the planets made of?

Astronomers are scientists who study objects in space. Little by little, they are piecing

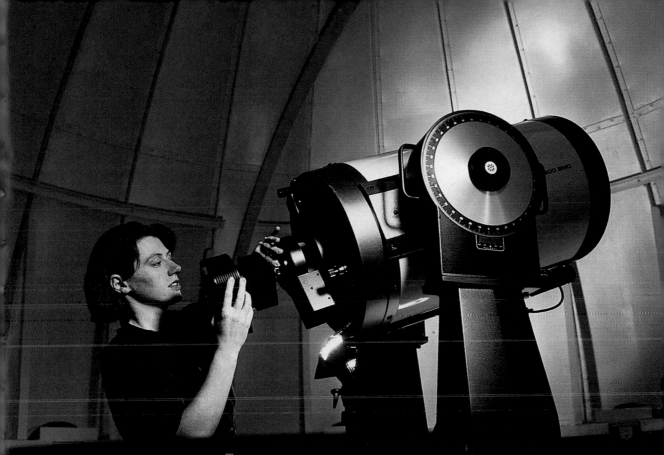

Astronomers use telescopes to study space.

the puzzle together. But the puzzle is very big and far from complete. Pieces of information are missing.

Studying Mercury will help astronomers understand the solar system.

Many astronomers believe that Mercury is a key piece to the puzzle.

The Planet Nearest the Sun

Mercury is the planet nearest the Sun. Like the other planets, Mercury travels around, or orbits, the Sun. It follows an elliptical path, like a stretched-out circle. Mercury's average distance from the Sun is about 36 million miles

Mercury is the closest planet to the Sun. Next come Venus, Earth, and Mars.

(58 million kilometers). This sounds as if Mercury is far, far away from the Sun. But Earth is even farther away. Earth's average distance is 93 million miles (150 million km).

People have known about Mercury since very early times. It is one of six planets that you can see with your eyes.

Early in the morning, Mercury can be spotted low in the sky.

(You need a telescope to see Neptune and Pluto.) Even so, Mercury is not easy to spot. It is small—only Pluto is smaller. It is also so close to the Sun that it gets lost in the Sun's bright glare. Dust and haze surrounding Earth make Mercury even harder to see. When Mercury is visible, it is low in the eastern sky just before sunrise or low in the western sky just after sunset.

The Winged Messenger

Very little was known about Mercury before telescopes were invented. Even without a telescope, Nicolaus Copernicus (1473–1543), a Polish astronomer, discovered that it takes Mercury just 88 Earth-days to orbit

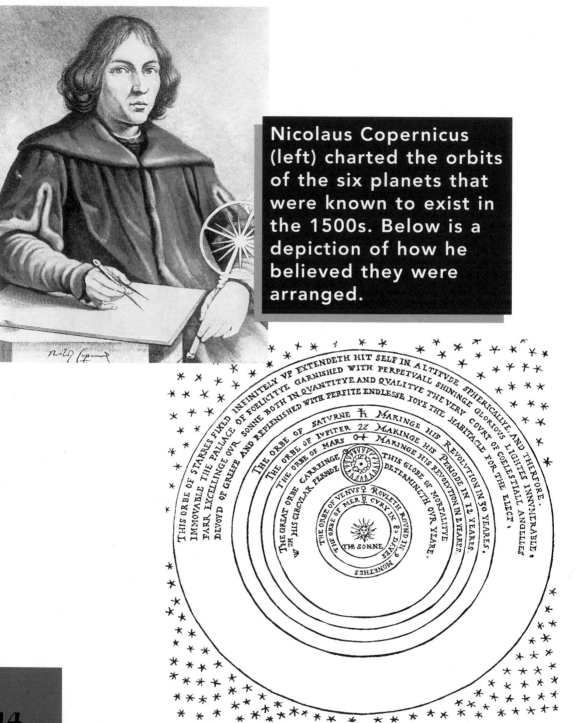

Nicolaus Copernicus (left) charted the orbits of the six planets that were known to exist in the 1500s. Below is a depiction of how he believed they were arranged.

the Sun. It takes Earth 365 days to travel around the Sun. This means that one Earth year equals 365 days.

How long is one Mercury year? If you say that a Mercury year is 88 Earth-days long, you are correct.

Mercury orbits the Sun more quickly than any other planet. For this reason, early observers named the planet after the Roman god who carried messages for the other gods.

The planet Mercury was named after the Roman god who was known to be speedy.

Mercury, or the winged messenger, was known for his speed.

New Ideas and Old Ideas

In the late 1950s, the United States and the Soviet Union began to explore the solar system. They sent probes, or spacecraft, to photograph and study the planets and their moons. The probes sent back information that told us more about the solar system than we had ever known.

The probe *Mariner 10* was an important tool for astronomers studying Mercury.

One probe, *Mariner 10*, zoomed past Mercury three times—in March and September 1974 and again in March 1975. Most of what we know about Mercury came from *Mariner 10*.

We knew some things about Mercury before *Mariner 10*. Copernicus had figured out the length of the Mercury year. In the 1600s, astronomers used the first telescopes to learn that Mercury goes through phases, just like our Moon. The Sun only

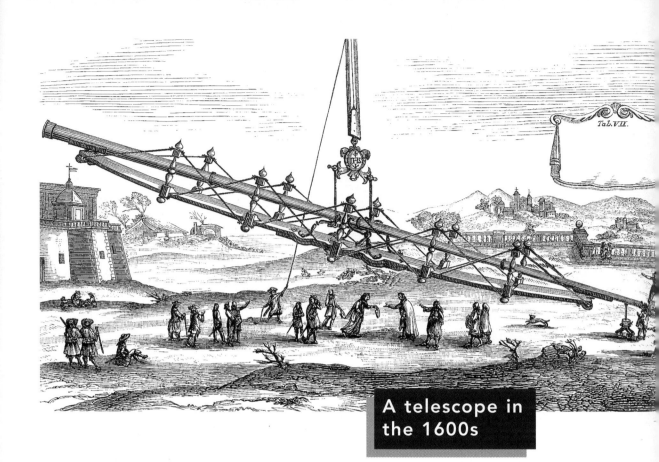

Tab.VII.

A telescope in
the 1600s

lights half of Mercury at a time.
Phases occur when we see only
part of Mercury's lit side.

Until 1965, astronomers
believed that Mercury did not

spin on an axis—an imaginary line about which a planet turns. They thought the planet always kept the same side turned toward the Sun. They were mistaken. After further study, they found that Mercury does spin, or rotate—but very slowly. It takes Mercury 1,408 hours to complete one rotation, or one Mercury day. It takes Earth only 24 hours to complete a rotation. Imagine 1,408 hours from one day to the next!

By Pull and

Mariner 10 was the first spacecraft to use the gravity of one planet to help it reach another planet. Gravity is the force that pulls objects toward a planet. As *Mariner 10* passed Venus, it used the pull of Venus's gravity to help it move faster toward Mercury. *Mariner 10* was also the first spacecraft to use the Sun's wind as a source of power. When its fuel ran low, *Mariner 10*'s solar panels were used like sails to catch the wind and help push the spacecraft along on its journey.

What We Know about Mercury

Mercury may be the second smallest planet in our solar system, but it is one of the most dense. Density is the measurement that tells us how light or heavy something is compared to its size. Mercury's density is 5.4. Earth's density

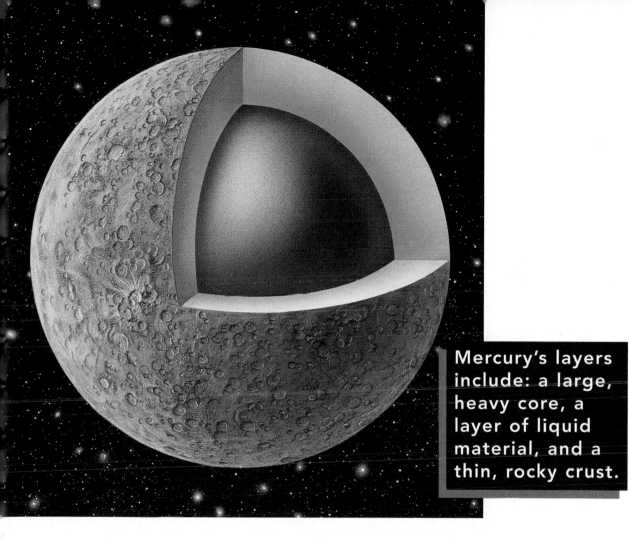

Mercury's layers include: a large, heavy core, a layer of liquid material, and a thin, rocky crust.

is 5.5, a little greater than Mercury.

Mercury is heavy because it has a large iron core. The

core is surrounded by a layer of liquid material, and this is covered by a thin, rocky layer.

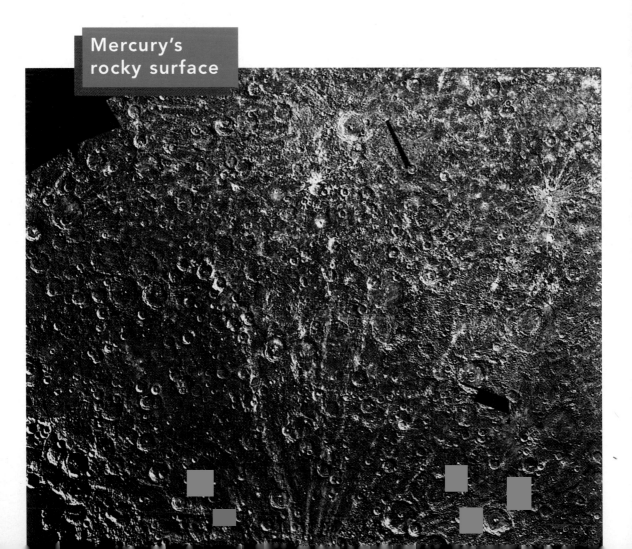

Mercury's rocky surface

Mercury is one of the rocky planets. Other rocky planets are Venus, Earth, Mars, and Pluto.

No one really knows why Mercury has such a large core. One theory, or explanation, is that Mercury crashed into another planet when it was quite young. The collision was so powerful that the cores of the two planets combined to create Mercury's large core.

Hot or Cold

Earth's atmosphere—the air or gas that surrounds our planet—is very thick. It acts like a blanket to keep the surface from becoming too hot or too cold.

Mercury has almost no atmosphere. Only a thin layer of helium and sodium gases

Mercury has almost no atmosphere. So its temperatures are either very hot or very cold.

surround it. So Mercury's temperatures are either very hot or very cold. Temperatures range from about 872 degrees Fahrenheit (467 degrees Celsius) during the long, sunny days to −298°F (−183°C) during the long, dark nights. Mercury has the greatest temperature range of any planet in the solar system. While half of Mercury bakes, the other half freezes!

A Many-Cratered Place

Mariner 10's pictures of Mercury look a lot like pictures of our Moon. This is because Mercury's surface is marked by craters, or holes. The largest of Mercury's craters is the Caloris Basin. It is 800 miles (1,300 km)

Craters cover
Mercury's surface.

wide and surrounded by moun-
tains up to 1 mile (1.6 km) high.
Some of Mercury's craters
were formed when Mercury

Meteorites are giant chunks of stone and metal.

was hit by gigantic chunks of stone and metal called mete-orites. Rocks thrown up by the meteorites crashed back

Comets are made of frozen water, gases, and space dust.

34

down and made other craters. Comets striking Mercury also created some of the craters. Comets are made up of frozen water, gases, and dust.

Unlike the Moon, Mercury's surface also has large areas of gently rolling plains. Cliffs, called scarps, crisscross the planet. Some are as high as 2 miles (3 km). Astronomers believe that Mercury's hills and scarps formed when it

Scarps, or cliffs, cut across the planet.

cooled and shrunk. Think of an apple that is left out to dry. Its surface becomes cracked and wrinkled. This is what scientists think happened to Mercury.

An area near the Caloris Basin has hills that are very different from the scarps. Scientists believe that the powerful impact that created the Caloris Basin made these hills, too.

Mercury Quick Facts

Diameter	3,031 miles (4,879 km)
Density	5.4
Average distance from the Sun	36 million miles (58 million km)
Surface temperature	872° to –298°F (467° to –183°C)
Length of day	59 Earth-days and 16 hours
Length of year	88 Earth-days
Moons	None

Missions to Mercury

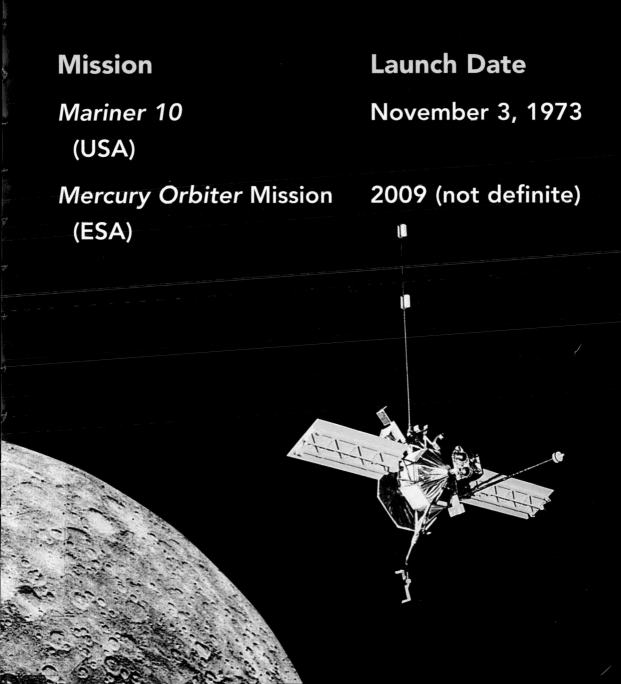

Mission	Launch Date
Mariner 10 (USA)	November 3, 1973
Mercury Orbiter Mission (ESA)	2009 (not definite)

The Future

Some astronomers think of Mercury as the forgotten planet because *Mariner 10* is the only probe that has ever flown by it. Also, *Mariner 10* looked at only half of the planet during its flights.

Has Mercury been forgotten? Perhaps not. The

Mariner 10 was only able to photograph half of Mercury's surface.

There are still many questions to be answered about Mercury. People will continue to look to the sky for answers.

European Space Agency (ESA) has been discussing possible plans for the *Mercury Orbiter* Mission. It may launch in 2009. The ESA hopes to discover things that *Mariner 10* missed. Will it? We'll have to wait and see. One thing is certain. Any future exploration of Mercury will add pieces to the puzzle of the solar system.

To Find Out More

Here are more places to learn about Mercury and other planets in space:

 **Books**

Asimov, Isaac. **Mercury, the Quick Planet.** Gareth Stevens Publishing, 1989.

Brewer, Duncan. **Mercury and the Sun.** Marshall Cavendish, 1993.

Simon, Seymour. **Mercury.** Morrow Junior Books, 1992.

Vogt, Gregory. **Mercury.** Millbrook Press, 1994.

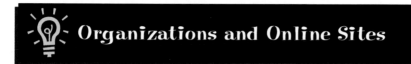
The Children's Museum of Indianapolis
3000 N. Meridian Street
Indianapolis, IN 46208-4716
(317) 924-5431
http://childrensmuseum.org/sq1.htm

Visit the SpaceQuest Planetarium to see what it has to offer, including a view of this month's night sky.

National Aeronautics and Space Administration (NASA)
http://www.nasa.gov

At NASA's home page, you can access information about its exciting history and present resources and missions.

National Air and Space Museum
Smithsonian Institution
601 Independence Ave. SW
Washington, DC 20560
(202) 357-1300
http://www.nasm.si.edu/

The National Air and Space Museum site gives you up-to-date information about its programs and exhibits.

The Nine Planets
http://seds.lpl.arizona.edu/nineplanets/nineplanets/

Take a multimedia tour of the solar system and all its planets and moons.

Space Telescope Science Institute
3700 San Martin Drive
Johns Hopkins University
Homewood Campus
Baltimore, MD 21218
(410) 338-4700
http://www.stsci.edu//

The Space Telescope Science Institute operates the Hubble Space Telescope. Visit this site to see pictures of the telescope's outer-space view.

Windows to the Universe
http://windows.engin.umich.edu/

This site lets you click on all nine planets to find information about each one. It also covers many other space subjects, including important historical figures, scientists, and astronauts.

Important Words

astronomer a scientist who studies objects in space

atmosphere the gases that surround a planet

axis an imaginary line about which a planet turns

comet a ball of frozen water, gases, and dust that orbits around the Sun

density the measurement that tells us how light or heavy something is compared to its size

elliptical shaped like a stretched-out circle

meteorite giant chunks of stone and metal that hit a planet's surface

orbit to travel around an object

rotate to spin

telescope an instrument that makes faraway objects look closer

Index

Meet the Author

Larry Dane Brimner is the author of more than fifty books for young readers, including these other titles in the True Book series: *E-mail, The World Wide Web,* and *The Winter Olympics.* He lives in San Diego, California.

Photographs ©: American Museum of Natural History: 14 top; Archive Photos: 20 (Kean Collection); Corbis-Bettmann: 14 bottom, 16; Greg Harris: 4–5; NASA: 1, 8, 26, 32, 33, 36, 38, 39 left, 41; Photo Researchers: 42 (Mark C. Burnett), 29 (Chris Butler), 25 (Lynette Cook), 2 (Dr. F. Espenak), 7 (James King-Hollmes/SPL), 34 (Jerry Lodriguss), cover (Mark Marten/NASA), 10 (SPL), 11 (Frank Zullo); UPI/Corbis-Bettmann: 18, 39 right.